The Work Book: A Practical Guide to Launching Your Career

Marianne Ruggiero

QUADERER
MEDIA GROUP

Quaderer Media Group
175 Varick Street
New York, NY 10014

The Work Book: A Practical Guide to Launching Your Career

Published by Quaderer Media Group
175 Varick Street, New York NY 10014
www.quaderer.com

First Edition: 2025
ISBN: 979-8-9916659-3-3 Paperback

Cover and book design by Emily CM Anderson

Library of Congress Control Number: 2025940194

For information about special discounts for bulk purchases, please contact info@quaderer.com.

Printed in the United States of America

Markets and economies change constantly, but the essential structure of the working world doesn't. *The Work Book* is a practical, hands-on guide to making sense of it all as you navigate the transition from school to work. You'll understand the structure of the marketplace, see how jobs and job functions relate, and learn how to forge a career path that's personally meaningful and professionally rewarding.

When you're through, you'll be able to answer fundamental career questions:

There are two basic types of jobs in the world. **Which type best aligns with your interests and talents?**

Depending on the path you choose, you can set yourself up for greater growth. **Which skills should you master to make yourself most valuable?**

Skills matter to your success, but where you work can matter even more. **Where are the best places for you to perform your job?**

Choosing the right first job helps set your trajectory. **What are the typical entry-level positions where you can get started?**

The Work Book is not about "following your bliss" and hoping for the best. It's about taking what you have and confidently, systematically turning it into a satisfying and successful work life from Day One.

Author's Note

When I launched my career consulting practice after many years of leading human resources departments at major companies, I worked out a clear, systematic, and informed way to help college students and recent graduates figure out what they wanted to do in life. This book is based on that work.

With The Work Book: A Practical Guide to Launching Your Career, you'll get a solid sense of how the market is structured and how it works—its dynamics, guiding principles, and the unwritten rules that shape careers. You'll learn how to match the kind of job you want with the sector and industry that aligns with your interests. And you'll see how to determine both your destination and the best starting point for getting there. This approach has helped hundreds of my clients, and I hope it proves just as useful to you as you read these pages.

Contents

4   FOREWORD

6   AN INTRODUCTION TO CAREERS

14   CHAPTER ONE
          Starting Out: Your Career in Your
          Twenties and Thirties

20   CHAPTER TWO
          The Four Career Paths:
          How You Get from Here to There

26   CHAPTER THREE
          Understanding the Job Market:
          Structure and Dynamics

42   CHAPTER FOUR
          Career Mapping: How to Narrow Interests
          and Industries

56   CHAPTER FIVE
          Your Best Fit: Finding the Right Job for You

72   CHAPTER SIX
          Launching: Initiating Your Job Search
          with Confidence

82   APPENDIX
          Suggested Reading and Key Resources

86   DEDICATION AND ACKNOWLEDGMENTS

Foreword

I always thought it was kind of crazy that the world—and certainly my parents—assumed that the minute you are handed your undergraduate diploma, you would somehow know exactly what you wanted to do for the rest of your life. Kudos to those very few who are able to figure that out before graduation, but most are not.

While we may have had a notion of what we wanted to do, most people starting out don't have a clue how to make it a reality. I would have saved much time and heartache if only I had had a practical guide of "news you can use" to help me on how to figure out what I really wanted to do. How can I take my interests and skills and turn them into not only a successful job search but the start of a wonderful career?

The good news is that my dear friend and advisor, Marianne Ruggiero, founder of Optima Careers, has written *The Work Book: A Practical Guide to Launching Your Career*, which should be required reading for every recent (and even the not-so-recent) college graduate. This clear and actionable guide helps you better understand how you fit into the work world and pinpoint your path intelligently, enabling choice and reducing the stress that can come with this process.

After successfully working with scores of clients over the years, Marianne has unique insight into the challenges recent graduates face. With her deep understanding of today's marketplace, *The Work Book* will give you the proven tools to set your course wisely as you begin to build your career.

And just as an aside, I did have a very successful

career. After a number of false starts in academic and magazine publishing, I found the field of Corporate Communications by accident, and it was a terrific fit. If I had worked with Marianne then, I probably could have skipped my adventure in publishing!

I spent the first three decades of my career working in increasingly senior communications roles at Chancellor Capital Management, *JPMorgan* Chase and Bank of America before pivoting to my dream job as Executive Vice President of Global Communications at The Estee Lauder Companies. During my thirteen-year tenure at Estee Lauder, Marianne was an invaluable coach and helped me successfully navigate a number of tricky mud puddles. I am incredibly grateful to her for her great wisdom, commonsense approach, tough love and deep empathy—I still owe you, dear Marianne!

I predict that you will feel a similar sense of gratitude after reading *The Work Book* and applying its lessons to your own career journey.

—Alexandra Trower

An Introduction to Careers

Setting career direction can be overwhelming. People avoid it for many reasons, including fear of the unknown or fear of being stuck with their decision forever. In my decades-long work as a career consultant, I've helped many, many young people launch their careers—people with different interests, aptitudes, skill levels, and dreams. While it may be challenging, you can overcome the obstacles, learn what you need to learn, and get on the right track.

To help you set *your* career direction, I have drawn on this work to create a simple and concise guide. This is not a philosophical guide or a booklet of self-help encouragement. It is a practical road map to give you a step-by-step approach to figuring out your career direction. Some chapters will reflect what you already know, some may feel counterintuitive, and others might give you an aha moment. But they are all based on universal truths about careers and the marketplace, and they form the foundation of an informed, satisfying process of discovery and exploration.

NOTHING TO FEAR

Let's mention a few more of those fears first, because it's helpful to hear that you're not alone. You might think that your major in college, such as Art History, will limit you to certain careers, like working in a museum or commercial art, and that it's too late to change direction. You may be feeling the paralysis that comes with hearing you're talented enough to do anything—endless options, but which one to choose? You might be searching for entry-level jobs and wondering which ones let you avoid grunt work and do interesting tasks instead.

If you're already in your first job, the fears can mount. Your job might seem interesting but have unclear expectations. Working and learning through trial and error is leading you to make mistakes. If you're not used to failing, work can feel like a minefield and become very stressful. Your colleagues might be decent enough people, but the camaraderie of school is missing. Unlike in college, where deep loyalties to one another are built, when someone in the office moves on, they are usually out of sight, out of mind. Maybe you were a star athlete and feel frustrated that those skills don't seem relevant to a professional career. School might have felt much easier to figure out. Your first job might quickly reveal that it's not what you had expected, and you might think you should stay for at least a year before moving on, as conventional wisdom suggests. This guide will help you push past these fears and frustrations to define a clear, individual path for yourself.

Ideally, you would have career direction and a professional job upon graduation. More likely, you are living at home and need to figure out what's next. At the same time, friends from school may be scattered around the country, so you're figuring out how to rebuild your social life. Dating is uncertain, your future is uncertain, and it's difficult to envision how it will all come together. The transition from student to professional, from dependent to independent, is much more challenging than most people expect. It becomes clear that you are responsible for designing and building your own life—socially, spiritually, emotionally, and financially.

WHAT'S YOUR FIRST NEXT STEP?

Let's consider three possible things you might do next: attend graduate school, take a gap year, or find a job. Graduate school is the easiest. There is a clear process for moving forward—but it is also the most expensive option. Taking a gap year, such as volunteering with the Peace Corps or Teach For America, can be worthwhile but delays the ultimate decision. Getting a job is the most difficult and least structured of these scenarios. Let's explore all three.

GRADUATE SCHOOL is the most obvious option. For careers requiring an advanced degree—and if you know with certainty that's what you want—then you should feel confident in continuing with your education. Social workers need an MSW, teachers may need a master's degree, and some nursing positions require an MS, for example. But check yourself to be sure that graduate school isn't, in fact, a delay tactic to defer your career decision. Studying international relations might be interesting, but if you don't speak a foreign language and aren't sure you want to be a diplomat, do you really need an advanced degree in the field? Instead, try test-driving a career track before investing time and money in graduate school. Before law school, try work as a paralegal or legal assistant; before committing to banking, do the pre-MBA two-year analyst program. In short, be sure an advanced degree is something you really need, not just something you think you want—or something to do next.

If you're considering an MBA (or even if you're not), ask yourself what skills it teaches. **Employers care less about the credential and more about the skills themselves.** For any career, having fundamental finance, accounting, and marketing knowledge and skills is valuable. Designing your own program based on an MBA course of study shows interest and initiative and adds value by giving you skills to enhance your résumé. What specific courses can you take to either qualify for an MBA program or to create your own program?

Parents often think an MBA is a good fallback option. But before applying, test the idea by designing your own personal MBA. Think about what you want to know about business, and build your own curriculum. Consider these essential courses:

1. Managerial Accounting (aka Cost Accounting): Managerial accounting provides the information needed to direct and control a business, including budgets, cost of products and services, product line profitability, and other relevant issues.

2. Marketing: Marketing has become quite broad, with creative-driven and quantitative marketing as well as traditional and digital marketing. **Balance your learning:** If you had a creative program in college, learn quantitative research methods; if you were quant oriented, take a class in design thinking. If you're digitally savvy, consider a course in brand marketing; if you are not digitally savvy, then look at courses in social media and related analytics to boost your skillset.

3. Financial Analysis and Strategy: Learn to analyze a business from the outside, understanding the perspectives of shareholders, investors, board members, and regulators. This involves thinking about an industry, market, economic trends, and the competitive landscape to project a strategic view of the business and the financials that inform strategy. Find a case study–method or game-based class in strategic management that involves financial analysis.

Regardless of which advanced degree you might decide to pursue, if you're still in college and have a lighter course load in your last semester or two, consider taking a Graduate Record Exam (GRE) prep course and the exam itself before you graduate. The scores are valid for five years, and if you decide later to apply to graduate school, your scores will be ready. You'll find it easier to take the test while still in "school mode."

A GAP YEAR (OR TWO) can be worthwhile if it has purpose and meaning. Participants in the Peace Corps and Teach For America are attractive to organizations because they demonstrate the ability to handle demanding situations requiring physical stamina, emotional fortitude, psychological strength, and mental agility. These programs build character and offer a strong alumni network to help in your career. If you want to explore the world, consider teaching English abroad and using your free time to work or volunteer in areas of job interest while advancing your language skills. These programs also help you explore, test, and develop functional skills.

I had a client with an undergraduate degree in creative writing who found a job in social work but didn't enjoy it. Prior to our consultation, he had been accepted to teach English abroad which would let him travel and buy time before setting his career direction. But before he left to teach, our work together led him to a decision to pursue landscape architecture. He ended up teaching English abroad, but also volunteered at a botanical garden to build a portfolio for graduate school applications. He pursued the degree, graduated, and launched a career in landscape architecture. He later started his own firm and credited that early thinking and strategizing for his career satisfaction and success.

The third option is to **GET A JOB**. This can be challenging, depending on your major, summer experiences, and skills. If you lack relevant experience, starting as an intern is fine. One of my clients interned at his college's investment office and stayed for a couple of years, which helped him transition into financial services. He wouldn't have broken into the field without that job, which taught him basic skills. And because he started at a place where people already knew him—at his college—he was given the benefit of the doubt as to his abilities. This is a good example of an important maxim: **People who know you will let you try something you've never done before. People who don't know you, won't.**

If you find jobs you're interested in but aren't qualified for, consider a boot camp or study program to bridge that gap. Vocational studies, once perceived as secondary to academic studies, are now valuable. A range of online companies and educational institutions offer courses, certificate programs, projects, and immersion programs. Universities have expanded their continuing education, certification programs, and alumni programs. Project management certification, for example, can boost your career by teaching specific knowledge, skills, tools, and techniques.

One of my clients graduated in Mechanical Engineering from the University of Edinburgh and moved to New York to find a job in financial services. We met after he had had six months of unsuccessful job searching. With me, he was willing to admit that he did not qualify for an analyst position and needed a different angle to get into the industry. We explored data science and identified the skills he'd need.

With some additional course work, he could qualify for internships. He took coding and accounting courses and shortly after qualified for an internship that put him on track for the career he had chosen.

Many, many life-defining moments happen early in your career, and your earning power is largely influenced in your first ten years of work. That means a lack of vision in your twenties can be costly. So, don't stay in a job where you're underemployed or doing something you don't enjoy. Find something that points you in the right direction from the start.

THE GUIDE

The chapters in this guide enhance your understanding of the market, provide practical insights, help you define your career direction, and give you more confidence in launching your career.

Chapter 1, "Starting Out: Your Career in your Twenties and Thirties", highlights key career questions for your twenties and thirties, helping you identify what's most important now. Chapter 2, "The Four Career Paths: How You Get from Here to There", describes typical career paths over time. Chapter 3, "Understanding the Job Market: Structure and Dynamics", educates you about market structure and dynamics. Chapter 4, "Career Mapping: How to Narrow Interests and Industries", addresses job types and functions, describing work you might want to perform. Once you've set career direction, chapter 5, "Your Best Fit: Finding the Right Job for You", helps you drill down into specifics before starting your job search. Chapter 6, "Launching: Initiating Your Job Search with Confidence", covers research and networking to align your interests with the market.

Throughout the chapters, you'll find important and universal career principles to reference as you navigate the transition from school to work. And the appendix offers some of the career-related books I recommend most often to my clients.

Let's get started!

CHAPTER ONE

Starting Out: Your Career in Your Twenties and Thirties

Each decade of your career is a distinct step in your professional evolution, where you will have specific decisions to make and goals to focus on.

YOUR TWENTIES

After college, you might choose to take a gap year—say, in the Peace Corps—or go to graduate school instead of heading straight into the working world. But eventually, you will transition to your first professional job.

In your twenties, you will face some age-old career questions:

1. Is there a workplace free of office politics?
2. Is it okay to take a job just for the money?
3. What should I specialize in?

First, I can assure you that there is no workplace without office politics. People can often make the workplace feel like high school or as if a few bad characters are out to get everyone. Instead of trying to avoid office politics, think of it as internally focused relationship building. If you reframe things this way, it will help you embrace office politics, and by doing so, you'll increase your chances of success (externally focused relationship building is what we usually refer to as " networking").

GUIDING PRINCIPLE

Relationship building focused internally is better known as "office politics"; relationship building focused externally is called "networking." Building a strong set of relationships inside and outside the office can be even more valuable than the actual work you produce. Relationships matter as much (if not more) than results. So stay in touch with the people you meet early on—many will be glad to know about your progress.

Taking a job just for the money is often a mistake. High pay can be a red flag. It might indicate a difficult boss or a dead-end job. Be sure to ask questions to understand why the job pays so well.

The most important question of the three is about specialization. The market rewards specialization. Spend your time and effort on developing competence in a specific job function, for example, marketing or operations.

GUIDING PRINCIPLE
Being smart, capable, and good at what you do is assumed. What sets people apart is persistence and soft skills—including consistency in communications and likability.

CASE STUDY: EMILY
One of my clients, Emily, had been a theater major and upon graduation started her career by managing fundraising events for a nonprofit cancer research organization. While she enjoyed the work, the environment wasn't all she had hoped for. When she heard about a marketing role with an online jewelry designer, she jumped at the chance to try something new. But it wasn't long before she realized that digital marketing wasn't for her. As we worked together, she figured out that her real passion was in healthcare and that her negative experience with her first job was symptomatic of that specific organization. She did some research and targeted top institutions with a broad range of fundraising activities. She landed two job offers, then chose one. She ended up happy with her work environment and continued advancing her skills.

In your twenties, you **focus on developing expertise.**

YOUR THIRTIES

In your thirties, you face three new career questions:
1. What additional skills do I need to increase my value?
2. How can I build my network and find a good mentor?
3. How can I ensure my compensation matches my level of contribution?

Increasingly, people are making major life decisions in their thirties—such as choosing a life partner, deciding if you want to have children, making lifestyle decisions about where to live and perhaps buying a home. In some regions or communities, these choices may come earlier, while in others, they may come later or take different forms. But by the time you are in your thirties, you are likely to have put down roots, both personally and professionally. It's the time to deepen your commitment to your field by developing relationships that will be important for long-term career growth.

Networking is not done only when you are job hunting; it helps you better perform the job you already have, because as you develop relationships in the market, you gain access to others' knowledge and experience. This helps you do your job with distinction, providing your organization with market insights and information. Mentors, who typically come from outside your organization and have no vested interest in what you do or don't do, provide objective feedback and make introductions.

And finally, in your late twenties and early thirties, having demonstrated the ability to add significant value, you correct any compensation shortfall. To successfully negotiate pay, you will need to know the specifics about how compensation works in your industry, in your function, and in your own company—and what jobs pay. Ask about your company's pay philosophy, market surveys, benchmark positions, and stock eligibility.

Your thirties also present two major challenges. The first is progressing beyond any programmatic milestones. For example, at a law firm, once you make partner it can be a bit more difficult to understand how you move from nonshare partner to equity partner or gain more shares. In banking, the path to VP is clear enough, but who makes managing director is shrouded in some mystery. The second key challenge is in your personal life: finding work-life balance, staying connected to your partner, and raising children of character. Mentors, colleagues and coaches can help you navigate these challenges.

GUIDING PRINCIPLE
You can have it all, just not at the same time.
Choose your priorities and accept the
consequences.

BEYOND JUST FINDING A JOB

Launching a career is not just about finding your first job. It's figuring out what you want to do, creating value for your employer through your mastery of skills, performing with distinction, and finding organizations where you have shared values and beliefs. Mastering a job function in your twenties prepares you for the exposure and connections you need in your thirties. So, focus on the present challenges, and build a strong foundation for your future.

NOTES

CHAPTER TWO

The Four Career Paths:

How You Get from Here to There

Navigating your career is like playing chess. The goal is to strategically manage your moves to achieve success. In chess, you manage your pieces, anticipating your opponent's moves. Strategy comes into play particularly with opening moves and then mastery of certain tactics throughout the game. You learn that there are sequences for moves that are optimal. Similarly, in your career, you try to follow strategies and tactics that have proven successful.

Learning from others about how they navigated their career is a great way to find out what works and what doesn't. However, it can be difficult to know what was random or unique in their story and what is universally true and applicable to everyone, including you. The best model for understanding career paths was developed in 1979 by Michael Driver and Ken Brousseau, professors at the University of Southern California. Their model features four possible paths: linear, expert, spiral and transitory. The **linear path** represents steady vertical growth within a single career field; the **expert path** focuses on mastery in a specific field, such as law, medicine, or academia; the **spiral path** involves developing skills over multiple roles, adding experience and expertise both to challenge oneself and to match evolving market demands; and the **transitory path** prioritizes variety and lifestyle choices over maximizing compensation.

These four paths have maintained their relevance over time, but before we go through them in detail, there have been some changes in the marketplace throughout the past few decades that need mentioning:

1. The shift in the employee–employer relationship: Individuals have learned to take ownership of their careers and are more likely to seek opportunities in different organizations to prove their value and provide some shield against mergers, restructurings and cost-cutting initiatives.

2. Globalization: Global markets have increased competition for jobs, from software engineers to graphic designers to customer service representatives.

3. Technology and digitalization: Career paths are reshaping rapidly as some professions shrink and new opportunities emerge—for example, robotics.

4. The transition to the gig economy: More people are self-employed freelancers and independent contractors filling roles once held by traditional employees.

5. The desire for innovation: Billions of dollars are invested in start-ups.

These changes have led to an even greater emphasis on expertise to ensure some level of career stability and resiliency.

Keep this in mind as we dive into the four career paths that Driver and Brousseau outline.

LINEAR PATH: Also known as "climbing the corporate ladder," the linear path involves progressing through successive levels of responsibility. As you advance, you may have to wait longer than you want to get to the next level and survive reorganizations that eliminate positions. You may have to make lifestyle sacrifices, such as moving to a different location and attending events in the evenings. When both you and your partner have careers, one may need to make the sacrifice for the other's advancement. What gives you staying power in this path is delivering a consistent, sustainable, high level of performance.

EXPERT PATH: Professionals are experts, such as lawyers, doctors, engineers, and designers. Experts are often motivated by knowledge. The expert path offers some security, as you become recognized for what you know and how well you do your job. You become the go-to person.

You may be thinking, "How can I know I will remain interested in this work for my entire work life?" You don't need to make a lifetime commitment. Your career can evolve; you can acquire additional areas of expertise to broaden your knowledge, allowing you to solve increasingly complex problems over time.

SPIRAL PATH: This pathway offers variety. You initially acquire expertise and competence in a given area and then embrace a new challenge in an area related to your core competency. People on this path seek new challenges for variety and growth. There is less support for this path because it may be more difficult and riskier. Also, people get used to you doing one thing and can hesitate when you want to try something else. But to the extent that you master new skills and add adjacent ones to your portfolio of accomplishments, you enrich both yourself and your market value.

There are many reasons why the spiral path is attractive. It lets you align with the market when starting out, then challenge yourself by developing new knowledge and skills. You can do this successfully if you maintain a consistent network. Some people choose to make a single pivot, while others do so more frequently, but it is typically in seven-to-ten-year increments. Examples are the scientist who becomes an astronaut or the lawyer who becomes a judge. This path is a progressive broadening of what you do, advanced by retaining who you know.

GUIDING PRINCIPLES

Major transitions take about three years. There is a runway to completing major career shifts—like transitioning from school to work. Learning how to make big transitions takes a lot of mental and emotional energy, so try to be patient with yourself and with others as you navigate your early career experience.

People who know you will let you try something you've never done before; people who don't, won't. If you want to expand your experience and try new things, people who know you will give you a shot because they trust you.

TRANSITORY PATH: This path is lifestyle driven, where you make choices for variety and novelty. The transitory path has no specific direction—you take turns wherever and whenever it suits you. People who pursue this path are motivated by commuting time, the social aspect of the workplace, work-life balance, and similar considerations. Barriers to entry are low. This path may result in lower pay and requires the ability to talk your way into opportunities. A real estate agent is a good example. Anyone can get a desk and phone at an agency and get licensed. But your financial success depends upon your ability to get listings. Many start, but few are successful.

You may think I've excluded a career path. Often, and with parental encouragement, young people choose the "path of exploration," whose motto is something like "Try anything and see what sticks." The upside is obvious—you get your career started—and you can always learn something that you'll use in the future. But the danger lies with your lack of commitment. The market prefers candidates who are committed to their task, organization, and products. Hiring managers aren't interested in supporting your shopping around for a career on their watch. And exploration often tells you more about what you *don't* want to do rather than helping you decide what you *do* want to do.

Many also ask about entrepreneurship. Entrepreneurs start organizations, but those organizations are founded to meet a market need. The people who work at a start-up bring capabilities in sales, marketing, product development, and the like. While many jobs at a start-up involve doing a lot of things, unless you learn how to do one thing well, it will be difficult to get another job elsewhere. If you take the start-up route, have a plan to develop specific skills and abilities in a specific job function.

YOUR CAREER PATH

You may be thinking about what the perfect path for you is. But in aiming for the perfect choice, you might lapse into confusion or inaction. The perfect career does not exist. The bottom line is that you must start somewhere, and that somewhere is answered in your response to this question: What should I specialize in? If you can answer that question with one of the four career paths in mind, all the better.

NOTES

CHAPTER THREE

Understanding the Job Market:

Structure and Dynamics

People often suggest networking as a way to gather information and seek advice about the job market. For many, though, the thought of networking is uncomfortable, and that's understandable. How can someone else know better than you what you want to do for a living? This leads many young people to search job postings online in hopes of stumbling upon an appealing position in the process. But after days (or weeks) spent winding through a labyrinth of listings, you might decide that relying on chance or fate probably isn't the best method. And you're right!

A much better way to kick-start your journey is to understand how the job market is structured. This structure doesn't change, so once you understand it, you'll always be better at focusing your job search, sourcing more useful information, asking better questions when networking, and making enduring career decisions—even course correcting if you need to.

Here are the essentials of the job market structure:

SECTORS

The job market can be divided into two main sectors: the public sector (commonly known as not-for-profit or nonprofit) and the private sector (for profit). The public sector includes organizations like churches, public schools, charities, clinics and hospitals as well as local, state and federal government, labor unions, museums, and libraries. These can be categorized into four distinct groups: Government, Education, Foundations, and Voluntary Agencies, all of which are nonprofit organizations and have tax-exempt status. They exist to provide public benefits or advance social causes. They typically operate with a long-term view while pursuing their mission.

PUBLIC SECTOR: GOVERNMENT

The public sector primarily refers to government-run organizations or agencies at the federal, state, and local levels.

Government jobs require passing a civil service exam and a specific application process that can take from six to eighteen months (posted online at USAJOBS.gov). Most federal jobs are in the executive branch under department heads in the president's cabinet. The legislative branch, which creates laws, offers staff roles that enable the offices of the House of Representatives and the Senate to function. The judicial branch, including the Supreme Court, interprets the law and is dominated by lawyers and their administrative support.

Most state jobs are in teaching, including aides and support roles in education, and then in protective services, including the police, firefighters and corrections officers. Local government jobs are posted on local websites and will typically include positions in education, the public library, and in local services such as sanitation.

Many new graduates are moving away from government jobs, especially at the federal level. Since 2000, the trend has been downward with only modest spikes (after 9/11 and Barack Obama's election in 2008). Shutdowns, pay uncertainty, and political pressure to reduce government-funded programs have all contributed to the declining interest in public service.

There are nongovernmental organizations (NGOs), also known as civil societies, that function independently of government, although they may receive government funding. They typically are organized on a community, national, or international level to serve social or political goals, such as humanitarian causes or environmental issues. Employment opportunities are few because these organizations are dispersed across the globe and the number of jobs is relatively limited given the pressure to put funds to use in the field rather than toward administrators. Examples of well-known NGOs include Save the Children with thirty national members based in London and Doctors Without Borders, based in France, which uses only 1% of its budget on management and general administration. The United Nations, a global membership organization, has a very specific recruiting path and includes an assessment exercise and a competency-based interview. A pool of candidates is presented to an independent review body composed of staff and management representatives who make a recommendation to the hiring manager.

PUBLIC SECTOR: EDUCATION

Education includes public and private institutions, with some career fluidity between the two. Teachers can move back and forth from public to private, but administrators have less flexibility. Within both public and private institutions, you can consider a range of levels from graduate school to undergraduate colleges, community colleges, vocational schools, secondary education, middle schools, and down to pre-K.

Essentially there are two kinds of jobs in education: teachers (who deliver education) and administrators (who manage the educational process and the facilities). Teachers are in great demand and in the future will need to be more digitally savvy. Today, more students have access to a computer and AI will continue to evolve the methods, efficiency and effectiveness of how teachers teach. AI will help teachers accommodate a broader range of learning styles and allow for more individualized instruction, for example, but only if teachers can master and leverage AI as they collaborate with students. While technology may make teaching jobs more exciting and impactful, fewer people are attracted to the field, discouraged by school violence, shrinking budgets and political influences in the classroom.

Teaching opportunities in higher education require a PhD for faculty positions, and administrators often have advanced degrees. Higher-education positions are highly desirable because of the attractiveness of campus life and the fact that compensation may include discounted or free tuition for family members. Jobs are relatively stable. There is some threat to this way of life in higher education because college and university governance is shifting from shared governance, where faculty and even students might have a voice in decisions, to a more corporate model where the board of trustees empowers the president to make decisions without necessarily consulting with other stakeholders, especially the faculty. This corporate model has caused discontent and even outright rebellion on some campuses.

If you do choose to work at a college or university, consider the governing model for that campus. Is it the more traditional shared-governance model or a more corporate structure that centralizes decision-making authority with the president and the Board of Trustees?

PUBLIC SECTOR: FOUNDATIONS

A private foundation provides grants and is sometimes called a 501(c). Generally, there are family foundations, private operating foundations, and corporate foundations. Due to IRS spending limitations (the annual expenditure for grants is 5% of assets, so most limit staffing costs at 2% of assets), job opportunities are relatively limited. Positions typically include an executive director, operations personnel, the general counsel, and grant makers who are responsible for distributing funds to worthwhile charities. Examples include the Ford Foundation, a behemoth with an endowment of $16 billion and 715 employees, and The Clark Foundation, a smaller organization with an endowment of $1 billion and fewer than one hundred employees.

In recent years, the purely altruistic motivation that once drove foundations has spawned philanthropic capitalism, which integrates business principles such as "return on investment" or "venture funding" into philanthropy. Grants are often large, multiyear, and targeted to specific causes such as education or healthcare. Examples include transformational foundations such as the Bill and Melinda Gates Foundation (a nonprofit) and CZI, the Chan Zuckerberg Initiative (an LLC, privately owned business) and the Audacious Project. From a career perspective, organizations that provide programs and services offer more career opportunities than foundations.

PUBLIC SECTOR: VOLUNTARY AGENCIES

These agencies are approved as nonprofits under section 501(c)3 of the IRS code and file their financial information with the state in which they are organized. Examples include the American Red Cross, the Road Runners Club, and Amnesty International. Professional associations like the American Bar Association and the Certified Financial Planners Association, which approves the credentials of financial planners, also fall into this category. Professional associations are relevant to the job market because they provide members with professional education, including certifications. Jobs in these organizations resemble those in business, but the jobs will have different titles, such as a "fundraiser" instead of "sales representative" or "account manager."

My clients frequently express concern about being unable to afford working for a nonprofit. However, I encourage them to reconsider this frequent bias. The larger the organization, the more likely you are to secure a good income. Smaller organizations may struggle to offer high salaries but offer flexible hours and pleasant working conditions to attract and retain talent, which can often appeal to those seeking a lifestyle-oriented career. Smaller non-profits also depend on individuals who are willing and able to make the trade-off between salary and dedication to a social cause. If you avoid the temptation to work for a small, struggling nonprofit and seek opportunities in larger organizations, you should be able to optimize your earnings.

To learn about nonprofit compensation, you can research the IRS Form 990, which lists the compensation of the highest-paid employees. This information is available on IRS website and at Pro Publica. If you go to irs.gov and do a tax-exempt organization search, it will allow you to select a database named Copies of Returns (990). You can then search by organization name to get the report.

PRIVATE SECTOR: FOR PROFIT

Understanding the private sector can be more complex due to its many industries. Different sources categorize industries differently, but lists from *Fortune*, *Forbes*, Dow Jones and Standard and Poor's offer valuable insights. One that I like is provided in McKinsey's newsletter: Energy and Materials, Advanced Industries, Consumer Goods & Retail, Financial Services, Professional Services, and Technology, Media and Telecom. An industry list is included in this chapter to help you focus on the most common industries for your career choice. Don't let the abundance of options overwhelm you. We're looking at the entire job market in this guide, but based upon your interests and where you live, you will be able to narrow your focus.

Industries are often concentrated in specific areas. For instance, the financial services industry is primarily based in New York City, historically known as Wall Street, with outposts in major US cities and around the world. Financial services broadly include accounting firms, banking, insurance, and family offices (the latter are private companies that manage a wealthy family's financial and nonfinancial needs). The hospitality industry has companies with headquarters spread across different cities and regions throughout the country, such as Airbnb in San Francisco, Four Seasons Hotels in Toronto, and Marriott in Maryland (just outside Washington, DC). Advancing within these organizations may require travel and relocation, possibly multiple times.

Power and influence tend to be concentrated in headquarters locations. Working at headquarters allows you to build relationships with top executives. However, working in a satellite office or working remotely may give you more autonomy. The trade-off of not working at HQ is that it may be more difficult to establish relationships at the most senior level and cross-functionally.

Industries have subsections, segments or tiers—the language changes by industry and is typically defined by customers. Consider whether you prefer working business to business (B2B) or working directly with consumers (B2C), or a combination of both. Transitioning between B2B and B2C can be challenging. Additionally, consider the difference between service-based industries and those that produce or sell tangible products.

Let's look at some examples. The apparel market, often referred to as retail, primarily operates as B2C. Price points vary significantly, with luxury brands such as Dior, Chanel and Hermès sold in department stores and brand-owned stores at the top and mass-market retailers like Target, Walmart, and The Home Depot selling lower-priced brands as private label at the lower end. Retail merchandisers—positions that determine product and pricing to drive revenue and meet profit targets—exist across the industry. However, a merchandiser at Gucci, which charges over $700 for high-end jeans, is not interchangeable with a merchandiser at Walmart selling $29 jeans. This is why transitioning between tiers and categories (luxury to mass, jeans to sweaters) can be challenging. It is generally easier to move down market but nearly impossible to move up market.

Banking tiers also illustrate this. Top-tier banks like Goldman Sachs, JPMorgan Chase, Morgan Stanley and Citi hold prominent positions in the market. The next tier includes foreign banks such as Nomura, Barclays, and Deutsche, followed by regional and local institutions. If you've been working for a foreign bank for more than five years, it will become increasingly difficult to secure a position at a top-tier bank. In essence, moving down market is possible, but moving up market is challenging.

CASE STUDY: MARCY

Another of my clients, Marcy, started her career in financial services and in human resources. After a few years, a recruiter approached her about a training and development opportunity with a law firm. The recruiter mentioned that Marcy might find law firms "too specialized," but the pay was attractive. Marcy eagerly interviewed and ultimately accepted an offer. Marcy was highly successful at the law firm but eventually wanted to return to financial services with more advancement opportunities. Marcy set her sights on global banks. After a year-long search, she had to admit that she lacked the competitiveness needed. She learned that while lawyers can move from law firms to in-house counsel positions, staff members face limited options. Her takeaway underscores a basic truth about jobs: the context—the setting—of the position matters.

A WORD ABOUT CONSULTING

Consulting is often recommended for those who are undecided about an industry. Consulting firms typically structure themselves by industry, as clients prefer consultants with specific knowledge of their market and customer. You are probably familiar with the large strategy firms such as McKinsey, Bain, and BCG, but there are many different types of consultants; for example, firms that consult in communications (Edelman), marketing (Ogilvy & Mather), and supply chain (Accenture). Some consulting firms, often identified as agencies, also provide tangible work product (SY Partners). Boutique firms may have a sector or industry focus. Consulting firms often employ a restrictive recruitment approach, limiting their on-campus recruitment to specific schools. If your school is not on their list, the likelihood of securing a position with them is less likely.

The Bridgespan Group, a firm founded by Bain Consulting, caters to nonprofits. It was created in part to provide an "internal sabbatical" opportunity for Bain consultants who wanted to travel less and work with a social mission for a period of time. After a tour of duty at Bridgespan, those consultants could return to Bain's core business.

NOTES

CONSIDERATIONS

As you make your decision regarding sector and industry, here are some of the factors to consider:

NONPROFIT	FOR PROFIT
Exists to achieve some higher purpose and serve humanity.	Exists to generate a profit and shareholder value.
Driven by increasing demand for services while funds decline; trend toward self-sustaining strategies to replace donations.	Driven by competition and gaining a competitive advantage.
Generalists (doing a little bit of everything)	Expertise and specialization.
Increasingly seeks out talent with business skills who can bring structure, order and a results orientation to the organization.	Leverages corporate social responsibility to enhance brand image, internally and externally (e.g., may designate one paid day off to perform community service).
Focuses on long-term results.	Focuses on immediate results.
Pace of change is slow.	Pace of change is fast.
You will meet C-suite executives.	You may never meet C-suite Executives.
Often behind in technology.	Invests heavily in technology.

NONPROFIT	FOR PROFIT
(continued)	*(continued)*
A bad day is when your client dies from abuse or an overdose.	A bad day is when the stock price goes down.
Effectiveness matters; there's pressure to raise money and spend as little as possible.	Efficiency matters; cost cutting is a way of life.
Professionalism is becoming increasingly more sophisticated, mirroring private sector.	Management and leadership competencies are valued, though this varies widely by industry and company.
People work there for some higher purpose, and they want to earn a decent living for their efforts—but accept a ceiling to compensation.	People work there because they need to earn a living and they want to make the most money possible—no ceiling to compensation.
Training and development resources may be limited, and you may have to pay yourself.	Training and development exist to serve business needs, and the organization pays.
Relatively little consolidation, minimal M&A.	Subject to mergers and acquisitions (M&A).

GOVERNMENT
Federal
Legislative (US Congress)

Executive Branch
Federal Agencies including:
Military • Office of
Management & Budget •
The Council of Economic
Advisors • The National
Security Council •
The White House

Judicial Branch
Federal Courts •
Supreme Court

STATE
Legislative Branch
Senate • State Assembly

Executive Branch
Education & Welfare •
Governor, Attorney General,
Comptroller • Public
Health & Safety • Roads &
Highways

Judicial Branch
Lower Courts •
Supreme Court

Local
Board of Elections •
Education, School Board •
Emergency Services •
Municipal Courts •
Parks & Recreation • Police
& Fire Departments •
Public Works • Town
Councils, Town Committee

Public Education
Higher Education • High
School • Middle School •
Elementary • Pre-K

FOUNDATIONS
**Philanthropic
Organizations**
Traditional Foundations •
Philanthropic Capitalism

**Private Operating
Foundations**
Museums, Zoos • Research
Facilities • Libraries

501(c)
Educational, Literary,
Scientific Research •
Religious Organizations •
Cemeteries

501(c) *continued*

Credit Unions ◆
Cooperatives ◆ Fraternities,
Sororities ◆ Recreation
Clubs ◆ Pensions, Trusts ◆
Professional Associations

Social & Voluntary Agencies

Churches ◆ Community
Based Organizations ◆
Hospitals ◆ Legal Aid ◆
Public Clinics

Non Governmental Organizations (NGOs) ◆

International ◆
Environmental Agencies ◆
Religious Organizations ◆
Relief Services

PRIVATE SECTOR: FOR-PROFIT INDUSTRIES

Natural Resources & Power
Agriculture ◆ Energy, Oil & Gas ◆ Forestry ◆ Metals & Mining ◆ Renewable Energy ◆ Utilities

Transportation & Logistics
Aerospace & Defense ◆ Aircraft Manufacturing ◆ Automotive & Transport

Manufacturing
Chemicals ◆ Computers ◆ Drugs, Pharmaceuticals ◆ Food Processing, Beverages ◆ Office Machinery ◆ Optical Goods ◆ Paper Goods ◆ Plastic, Paint, Glass, Metal ◆ Soap, Perfume, Cosmetics ◆ Textiles, Apparel, Furniture

Equipment / Leasing
Agricultural Equipment ◆ Aircraft, Shipping, Vessels ◆ Business, Retail & Office ◆ Construction ◆ IT Equipment ◆ Medical Technology

Consumer Packaged Goods
(CPG), Retail & Wholesale

◆ Apparel, Home Goods
◆ Auction Houses, Galleries
◆ Beauty / Cosmetics
◆ E-commerce ◆ Education
◆ Food & Beverage

Travel & Hospitality
Amusement ◆ Gaming & Casinos ◆ Health Clubs, Gyms ◆ Hotels, Restaurants ◆ Private Clubs ◆ Golf Courses ◆ Recreation, Theme Parks ◆ Travel

Media, Entertainment & Sports
Digital Publishing ◆ Gaming, Games ◆ Film, Music, Video, Audio ◆ Live Events, Tours, Theaters ◆ Radio, Television, Cable ◆ Social Media ◆ Sport Teams, Associations ◆ eSports ◆ Text & Book Publishing ◆ Streaming Services ◆ Talent Management

Technology & Telecom
Artificial Intelligence ◆ Biotech ◆ Consumer Electronics ◆ Data / Intelligence Applications ◆ Hardware, Software ◆ Household Appliances ◆ IT Services ◆ Telephone, TV, Internet Providers

Healthcare
Ambulance Services ◆
Care Facilities, Elder
Care ◆ Health Services
(PT, Nutrition) ◆ Home
Health Services ◆
Hospitals (for profit) ◆
Mental Health Services ◆
Pharmaceuticals ◆ Private
Medical Practices ◆
Residential Facilities

Real Estate & Construction
Appraisal ◆ Brokerage
◆ Commercial Development
◆ Investment, Asset
Management ◆ Property
Management ◆ Residential
Development

Financial Services
Asset Management ◆
Alternative Asset
Management ◆ Blockchain
/ Crypto ◆ Commercial
Banking ◆ Consumer
Banking ◆ Exchanges—
Stock, Commodities ◆
Insurance & Reinsurance ◆
Investment Banking ◆ Private
Equity, Venture Capital ◆
Wealth Management

Professional Services
Consulting ◆ Accounting ◆
Economic Advisory ◆
Government Services ◆

Human Resources ◆ ◆
Recruitment & Staffing ◆
Compensation & Benefits ◆
Management & Leadership ◆
Legal ◆ Operations, Supply
Chain ◆ Regulatory &
Compliance ◆ Strategy

Security Services
Cybersecurity ◆ Security
Systems ◆ Security Guards

Outsourcing Services
Accounting, Billing ◆
Customer Service ◆
Data Services ◆ IT
Management ◆ Marketing ◆
Shipping & Logistics

Marketing
Advertising ◆ Affiliate ◆
Branding ◆ Channel ◆
Content ◆ Digital ◆ Direct
Marketing ◆ Experiential ◆
Events ◆ Licensing ◆
Market Research & Insights ◆
Membership / Loyalty ◆
Partnerships ◆ Performance
◆ Product Marketing ◆
Social Media

Communications
Communications Strategy ◆
Government Relations ◆
Investor Relations ◆ Media
Relations ◆ Political
Consulting ◆ Public Relations

CHAPTER FOUR

Career Mapping: How to Narrow Interests and Industries

Entering the job market can feel daunting, disorienting, and overwhelming. It has its own order and patterns, which you can learn and use to your advantage. Understanding the world of jobs—the job market ecosystem—allows you to combine your self-awareness with a clearer sense of where to find the career you want. It's like visiting a new city: Initially, you go to areas you've already known about, similar to limiting your job search to open positions. But once you get a map, you start to explore new neighborhoods.

An ecosystem is a structure that overlays an environment to help demonstrate and make sense of how different members and components function together. It is similar to ecosystems in the natural world you might learn about from *National Geographic*, which show the interconnectedness of plants, animals and other organisms operating in a single, living community. It is fascinating to understand their interaction and interrelationships—just as it is to learn about the nonliving community of soil, air, and water. Understanding your work environment as an ecosystem gives you more control over your goals, plans, and activities. Boris Groysberg's research, detailed in his book *Chasing Stars*, highlights how much context matters. Star performers in an industry don't develop in a vacuum; their performance relies heavily on their situation and environment.

The job market is an ecosystem comprising related players—customers, organizations, suppliers, and consultants—working together in a marketplace. As in nature, there are threats and opportunities triggered by new products, services and players. Economic and world events impact the market—just remember how the pandemic in 2020 accelerated a preference for remote working and devalued commercial real estate. Your challenge is to enter and navigate this ecosystem effectively.

By mapping the ecosystem of your chosen sector and industry, you can identify where you might work and think strategically about trends, political implications, regulations, infrastructure issues, research, innovations and scientific breakthroughs that will impact your future.

HERE'S A GENERAL MAP OF A BUSINESS ECOSYSTEM

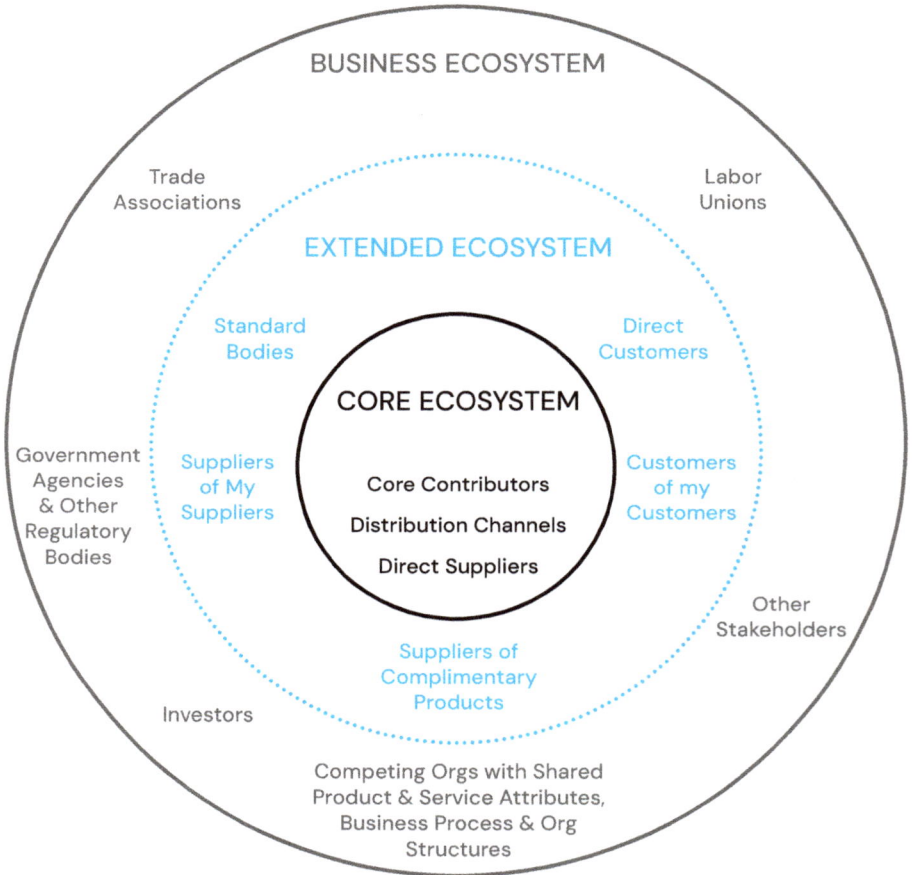

BUSINESS ECOSYSTEM

Trade Associations

Labor Unions

EXTENDED ECOSYSTEM

Standard Bodies

Direct Customers

CORE ECOSYSTEM

Core Contributors

Distribution Channels

Direct Suppliers

Suppliers of My Suppliers

Customers of my Customers

Government Agencies & Other Regulatory Bodies

Other Stakeholders

Suppliers of Complimentary Products

Investors

Competing Orgs with Shared Product & Service Attributes, Business Process & Org Structures

Based on James F. Moore, *The Death of Competition*, John Wiley & Sons, 1996.

AI is helpful for getting an ecosystem breakdown of any industry you're interested in. For music, you might try the prompt "Create a comprehensive ecosystem map for the music industry."

Here's the ecosystem map you would get in return:

1. Artists and Creators: Musicians • Singers • Songwriters • Producers • Composers • DJs • Bands

2. Production and Recording: Recording Studios • Mixing Engineers • Mastering Engineers • Music Producers • Sound Engineers

3. Distribution and Sales: Record Labels • Major Labels (e.g., Universal Music Group, Sony Music, Warner Music Group) • Independent Labels • Digital Distribution Platforms • Streaming Services (e.g., Spotify, Apple Music, Tidal) • Online Music Stores (e.g., iTunes, Amazon Music) • Social Media Platforms (e.g., YouTube, TikTok) • Physical Distribution • CD and Vinyl Manufacturers • Retail Stores (e.g., HMV, Walmart) • Online Retailers (e.g., Amazon)

4. Marketing and Promotion: Public Relations Firms • Music Promotion Agencies • Social Media Influencers • Music Blogs and Websites • Radio Stations • Television Networks • Music Video Directors

5. Live Music and Touring: Concert Promoters • Booking Agents • Tour Managers • Event Planners • Venue Owners / Operators • Ticketing Platforms (e.g., Ticketmaster, Eventbrite) • Sound and Lighting Technicians

6. Music Publishing and Rights Management: Music Publishers • Rights Management Organizations • Performing Rights Organizations (PROs) (e.g., ASCAP,

BMI, SESAC) • Mechanical Rights Organizations (e.g., Harry Fox Agency) • Synchronization Rights Organizations • Copyright Lawyers

7. Fan Engagement and Community: Fan Clubs • Music Festivals • Music Awards and Competitions • Merchandise Companies • Patreon and Crowdfunding Platforms

8. Education and Development: Music Schools and Conservatories • Online Music Education Platforms (e.g., MasterClass, Coursera) • Workshops and Masterclasses • Mentorship Programs

9. Technology and Innovation: Music Production Software Companies (e.g., Avid, Ableton, FL Studio) • Music Hardware Manufacturers (e.g., Fender, Gibson, Yamaha) • Music Tech Start-ups (e.g., SoundCloud, Bandcamp) • Artificial Intelligence and Data Analytics Companies

10. Legal and Financial Services: Entertainment Lawyers • Accountants and Financial Advisors • Insurance Providers • Contract Negotiators

Going further, use the prompt "Create a list of key relationships and interactions in the music industry." You'll get something like this:

1. Artists and Creators: Interact with **Production and Recording** to create music • Directly engage with **Marketing and Promotion** for visibility and fan engagement • Depend on royalties and intellectual property protection • Perform through **Live Music and Touring** to connect with fans and generate revenue.

2. Production and Recording: Work with **Artists and Creators** to produce high-quality music • Provide finished music to Distribution and Sales for market release.

3. Distribution and Sales: Distribute music created in **Production and Recording** to various platforms • Partner with **Marketing and Promotion** to boost sales and streaming • Collaborate with **Music Publishing and Rights Management** to ensure proper licensing and royalties.

4. Marketing and Promotion: Promote music through various channels, enhancing visibility for **Artists and Creators** • Collaborate with **Distribution and Sales** to drive sales and streams • Engage with **Fan Engagement and Community** to build a loyal audience.

5. Music Publishing and Rights Management: Manage rights and royalties for **Artists and Creators** • Ensure legal use of music through **Distribution and Sales** • Collaborate with **Marketing and Promotion** to maximize revenue • Support **Live Music and Touring** by managing performance rights.

6. Live Music and Touring: Provide platforms for **Artists and Creators** to perform live • Generate revenue and promote music through performances • Engage with **Fan Engagement and Community** directly.

7. Fan Engagement and Community: Build and maintain a loyal fan base for **Artists and Creators** • Interact with **Marketing and Promotion** to keep fans updated. • Enhance the live experience through **Live Music and Touring**.

8. Education and Development: Develop future **Artists and Creators** and industry professionals. • Provide training and skills development in Production and Recording and other areas • Integrate with **Technology and Innovation** to teach new methods and tools.

9. Technology and Innovation: Develop new tools and platforms for **Production and Recording** • Provide innovative solutions for **Distribution and Sales** • Enhance fan experiences and engagement through new technologies.

10. Legal and Financial Services: Provide legal support for contracts, rights management, and disputes • Offer financial advice and services to manage revenue streams • Ensure compliance across all interactions within the ecosystem.

Then, ask for the names of three companies for each area, to start a target list for a job search:

KEY AREAS WITH COMPANY EXAMPLES (2024)

1. Artists and Creators: Musicians: Beyoncé, Ed Sheeran, Billie Eilish • **Bands:** Coldplay, Imagine Dragons, Foo Fighters • **DJs:** Calvin Harris, David Guetta, Marshmello

2. Production and Recording: Recording Studios: Abbey Road Studios, Electric Lady Studios, Capitol Studios • **Music Producers:** Max Martin, Rick Rubin, Pharrell Williams • **Mixing/Mastering Engineers:** Chris Lord-Alge, Tom Coyne, Emily Lazar

3. Distribution and Sales: Streaming Services: Spotify, Apple Music, Tida • **Online Music Stores:** iTunes, Amazon Music, Bandcamp • **Physical Retailers:** Walmart, HMV, Target

4. Marketing and Promotion: PR Firms: 42West, Nasty Little Man, MBC PR • **Promotion Agencies:** The Syndicate, Co-Sign Planetary Group • **Social Media Influencers:** Logan Paul, Liza Koshy, Lele Pons

5. Music Publishing and Rights Management: Publishers: Sony/ATV Music Publishing, Universal Music Publishing Group, Warner Chappell Music • **Performing Rights Organizations:** ASCAP, BMI, SESAC • **Mechanical Rights Organizations:** Harry Fox Agency, Music Reports, Loudr

6. Live Music and Touring: Concert Promoters: Live Nation, AEG Presents, C3 Presents • **Booking Agents:** Creative Artists Agency (CAA), William Morris Endeavor (WME), United Talent Agency (UTA) • **Ticketing Platforms:** Ticketmaster, Eventbrite, StubHub

7. Fan Engagement and Community: Fan Clubs: BTS Army, Beyoncé's Beyhive, Lady Gaga's Little Monsters • **Music Festivals:** Coachella, Glastonbury, Lollapalooza • **Music Awards:** Grammy Awards, MTV Video Music Awards, Billboard Music Awards

8. Education and Development: Music Schools: Berklee College of Music, Juilliard School, Musicians Institute • **Online Education Platforms:** MasterClass, Coursera, Berklee Online • **Workshops and Masterclasses:** Red Bull Music Academy, Grammy Museum, Songwriting Camps

9. Technology and Innovation: Production Software: Avid (Pro Tools), Ableton (Live), Image-Line (FL Studio) • **Hardware Manufacturers:** Fender, Gibson, Yamaha • **Music Tech Start-ups:** SoundCloud, Bandcamp, Splice

10. Legal and Financial Services: Entertainment Law Firms: Grubman Shire Meiselas & Sacks, King & Ballow, Pryor Cashman LLP • **Accounting Firms:** Music Industry Accounting, FBB & Co., Dunn Pariser & Peyrot • **Insurance Providers:** MusicPro Insurance, Aon/Albert G. Ruben Insurance, Hencilla Canworth

Luma, which specializes in digital media and marketing, is known for their "LUMAscapes," which are visual representations that categorize companies within the digital ecosystem, helping to clarify the complex relationships among various entities in the industry. Here's a simplified example of a LUMAscape:

© LUMA PARTNERS LLC 2025

IF YOU NEED TO CREATE YOUR OWN MAP, FOLLOW THESE STEPS:

STEP 1. Identify the players. Players are those who have a stake or interest in the organization. Make a list of those central to an organization you're focusing on—customers, people who have an interest or gain by connecting within the system, people who solve the same problem, and people who create products and services that aid that market. Include opponents, competitors, government agencies, influential bystanders, etc. For example, Apple will have its detractors, such as people who are critical of compliance with Chinese censorship or may criticize Apple's walled-garden approach.

Instead of asking "What job do I want?" start with "What problem do I want to solve?" Consider who is involved in solving that problem and where you could add value and have impact.

STEP 2. Identify the environmental conditions. List the politics, new laws, regulations, economies, social norms or cultural ties, research organizations, or relevant studies at labs or universities that impact the ecosystem. Consider market economics as well as dominant players. Identify beliefs or values at play, such as a history of inclusion or exclusion.

STEP 3. Create your map. You can draw it out on a piece of paper. Start with the customers: Who are they, and whom do they go to for this product or service? Track the flow of transactions with arrows. Tools are available online to aid in your mapping, and it can be helpful to do this with a friend who's creating their own map. Compare your maps as you go, inspiring each other as you brainstorm together.

STEP 4. Develop insights and generate ideas for job possibilities. Consider the information on your map, and start to form ideas about what it could mean for you. Identify important job functions that cross all stakeholders, dilemmas, and opportunities. Determine what conditions need to change for progress to happen and what new innovations or functions could have a positive or negative impact.

Think about where you could establish the most credibility and have the highest impact on the customer or support an organization's competitive advantage. Assess the talent pool—how saturated is it, and how competitive would you be in that environment? All of this will involve some research into roles and consideration of how they operate together to make work happen.

To think about stakeholder interactions, understand that they can be categorized into buyers and sellers (or buy side and sell side) of transactions. For example, McKinsey sells consulting services but also buys technology services.

For a good example of these interactions and their implications for career navigation, consider the retail market in marketing. You can start on the sell side (e.g., an agency such as AKQA) and move to the buy side (e.g., a company like Nike). Buy-side jobs involve marketing to consumers (B2C), while sell-side roles involve marketing to businesses (B2B). Expertise and skills differ between these sides, influencing career path and responsibilities. It is unusual to go from the buy side (Nike) to the sell side (AKQA) because the knowledge and skills required are not the same. The "experts" are on the sell side; your development puts emphasis on developing expertise and applying that to a broad range of customers while also requiring business development and selling skills.

If you start in marketing at Nike, you will advance within the marketing function, starting as an assistant or coordinator or specialist. Along the way, you manage marketing campaigns based upon your understanding of the Nike customer. At some point you will be involved in buying media, and you'll do that through agencies, including AKQA. On the buy side, you're learning how to negotiate and evaluate vendors, making decisions about whom to hire and managing the services purchased.

You could argue that you must "sell" in every job, but on the sell side you have the responsibility to generate revenue. For example, if you work for a consulting firm, you will have billable hours, meaning your specific work brings in money (revenue) for the company. It is a job with P&L (profit and loss) responsibility. If you start at an agency, you'll be an account coordinator or assistant and advance to Account Management, ultimately becoming a Partner. Along the way, you'll be involved in business development. Managing multiple accounts, upselling, and managing the P&L of agency work requires different skills and abilities than the marketing executive working in house on a specific brand and product category. On the sell side, you are selling and partnering with customers to help them generate revenue, provide infrastructure or reduce expenses.

The concept of buy side and sell side applies to nonprofits as well. For example, the buyer is the client that benefits from your organization's programs. The nonprofit organization is the seller, offering up its programs or services, even though they may be free or be provided at a nominal cost. The American Red Cross is a global nonprofit offering programs and services around the world. They are "selling" their services and organizations, and individuals buy (or benefit from) their offerings. If you are raising money for a nonprofit, you're selling the mission and services of your organization to funders or donors, who are buying into your mission and services by giving away their money to your charity or cause. But if you hire an outside fundraising company to help you, you're the buyer and the consultants are the sellers.

With a detailed understanding of your desired marketplace, you can further explore the kinds of jobs that exist and how they fit into your chosen ecosystem.

Use the map to identify organizations to explore, regardless of immediate openings. By working to connect with people there before jobs open, you'll be on their radar and known for future opportunities.

NOTES

CHAPTER FIVE

Your Best Fit: Finding the Right Job for You

The job market rewards specialization, so it's useful to define your career direction first by job function (the tasks you perform) before considering the context (the sector or industry where the job is located). Expertise is what gives you earning power, and the sooner you develop it, the sooner you create value and improve your pay.

In choosing an area of specialization, it's helpful to understand the organizational structure that is common across sectors. However, also know that similar functions have different names depending upon their sector. For example, a key profit and loss (P&L) position in a consumer packaged goods company (CPG) is called a Brand Manager. A similar role in technology is called a Product Manager—while in financial services, a Product Manager is an entirely different job. In retail and fashion, the P&L job might be called a Buyer or Merchandiser, and in nonprofit it's called a Program Manager.

Your goal is to find the right combination of job function and industry. You need to know what you want and how to name it—otherwise, you'll be stuck in endless exploration. Start by choosing one of two job types: line or staff.

LINE JOBS

Line jobs drive revenue, while staff jobs support those who generate revenue. In Europe, line jobs are referred to as "revenue generating" and staff as "revenue enabling." In entertainment, you may hear about jobs as "above the line" or "below the line." Some organizations refer to line jobs as "front office" or "essential." The most obvious line jobs are in Sales, but many Marketing positions are also line. In financial services, they call line jobs "front office" and staff jobs "back office" (and to add to the confusion, they also have a "middle office," implying some client-facing responsibilities but shy of direct revenue generation).

People associate several characteristics with line positions. If you have an outgoing personality and are self-confident, people will suggest Sales. But looking more deeply, it also aligns well with people who are organized, good at time management, and like to work independently. You need good social skills, including the ability to pick up on verbal cues and listen attentively. Salespeople need to know their product or service extremely well, so you need to have some inherent interest in the product or service you sell. Relationship-driven selling requires that you be able to establish trust and cultivate relationships, are knowledgeable about your customer's business, and can track details of their account. You must be willing to ask for the sale, including knowing when and how to upsell. You need to understand the sales process and, in many cases, be confident in delivering sales presentations or pitches. Knowing how to close a sale or deal is important, and that might include negotiation skills. Finally, it may take a lot of calls, from cold calls to scheduled appointments, to sell your product or service. You will be expected to call on a number of customers, and many may reject you, so you need to have a relatively resilient personality.

Often I hear young people say that they are not interested in sales. They are usually imagining the old cliché of the shady used car salesman who is hiding any information about the car that might dissuade you from purchasing. When I reframe sales as the ability to influence others, they're more interested. Some are willing to consider sales when the title is more refined—such as Account Executive, Account Manager, Customer Success Specialist, etc. Many marketing jobs are line jobs. Again, the criterion is revenue generation. If you work at American Express and market cards to consumers, you're in a line job. If you do cause-related marketing or sponsor events, then your work does not directly drive revenue and it's not a line job.

If you work at a nonprofit and raise money, the position might be called Advancement or Development. You are asking people to donate money to your cause, and when they write out a check, you've raised money—so it's a line job. If you develop programs or events and charge a fee, it's a line job.

In some organizations, there is staff that support sales, reports into sales and often includes client-facing responsibilities. These are sometimes referred to as "middle office" jobs. Financial services is well known for having a middle-office function. How would you know if the position you're considering is middle office or front office (or not)? By knowing where the department reports. If the position reports into Sales, then it's middle office and you could be on track for a line role. If the position reports to Operations, then you're on track for a staff role.

The people who create product may not directly bring in sales, but they are essential because without product, there is nothing to sell. In a fashion company, the Designer (the product is essential), the Merchandiser (who prices and makes the product is essential), the Store Associates and ecommerce merchandisers are line positions.

STAFF JOBS

Staff positions support the revenue generators. They are often associated with individuals who are motivated by power through influence, comfortable with performance evaluations based on qualitative measures, have a passion for helping others, and thrive on improving products, processes, or people. They are often exceptionally adept at working with diverse personalities.

Some characteristics of people well suited to line and staff jobs:

LINE	STAFF
Direct responsibility for achieving revenue goals (P&L responsibility)	Supports those who drive revenue
Decides; lots of stamina	Influences, suggests, recommends
Commercially oriented	Service oriented
Low need for acceptance or approval	May prefer to avoid failure or criticism
Power looks like competence and achievement	Power looks like competence, influence and achievement
Willing to confront others, be aggressive	Willing to find common ground
Leads and controls; willing to have everyone else's mortgage on their shoulders	Leads and supports; willing to help everyone else be successful
Willing to fail, risk tolerant; not dissuaded by challenge and adversity	Willing to serve, risk avoidant; challenge and adversity are inevitable

CASE STUDY: CHRISTIAN

I had another client, Christian, who was a rising senior in college with an interest in music and games. He wanted to specialize in something that would allow him to be creative, work independently, and avoid multitasking. We focused on mobile gaming and researched to identify a job function for which he had an interest and could qualify. Product Development, Production, and Marketing offered everything from playing games to finding bugs to designing content and acquiring users. He decided to target Marketing and identified entry-level positions in customer service.

HOW TO CHOOSE A JOB FUNCTION

Christian's story illustrates how knowing the essential job functions enables you to align your interests and skills more easily to an area of specialization. Many people choose an industry first and don't put enough emphasis on what work they'll do when they arrive—a big mistake.

Another way to approach choosing a job function is to refer to the organization chart provided here as a reference. The chart indicates the job functions that you would typically find in any organization, even if the exact names may vary by industry. The essential job functions include Sales, Marketing, Product Development, Operations, Technology, Finance & Accounting, Communications, General Counsel and Human Resources.

If you have determined that you are suited to line positions, then you will focus on positions that directly impact generating revenue, sales and marketing. If you decide on staff positions as the better fit, then you would look toward functions that primarily deal with product, data, or people.

All jobs require a certain level of interpersonal skills, critical thinking, and good communications skills. So, **61** knowing that you want to work with people or with data is also somewhat helpful in identifying the job function. Think about your potential skill level as well—if you have good communications skills, do you have the interest and potential to develop exceptional skills? If so, you might consider becoming a communications consultant or lawyer.

I can't emphasize enough the importance of becoming great at what you do. The person who gets things done and who is great at what they do will have opportunities, so choose something where you can be all in.

FOLLOWING ARE SUMMARIES OF EACH KEY FUNCTION:

SALES: Generates revenue; identifies, engages, and develops customers or clients. Titles include Brand Sales Specialist, Customer Success Manager, Director of Global Strategic Alliances. In nonprofit, the "sales" jobs are typically called Development or Advancement.

BUSINESS DEVELOPMENT (BD): Sometimes a function of sales or may operate separately. BD is about developing business opportunities and cultivating commercial relationships—for example, potential sponsorships, partnerships or other initiatives that would serve both parties, exploring new markets. It might be prospecting for new clients that are handed over to sales for execution.

MARKETING: Creates strategies to promote products or services, build and enhance the brand, and attract new customers while integrating brand management (P&L), branding, research (data science), digital and traditional advertising, public relations, social media management, and content creation. Titles include Brand Manager, Product Manager, Pricing Manager, or Program Manager.

PRODUCT MANAGEMENT / PRODUCT DEVELOPMENT: Creates, designs, and prototypes new products and services. This could be the denim designer at Ralph Lauren or the AI Engineer at Google. A Product Manager (PM) has P&L responsibility and, if the product is highly technical, is likely to have come from engineering. If the product is not so technical, then the PM is likely to come from marketing. The PM works with marketing to understand what the consumer wants and then works with the engineers to build that product.

OPERATIONS: Ensures that day-to-day activities are executed well. This may include production, manufacturing, logistics, supply chain, and quality control. Operations teams are often focused on improving efficiency, reducing costs, and managing product or service quality. Subdepartments may include Quality Assurance, Purchasing, and Inventory Control.

DATA AND INFORMATION TECHNOLOGY: Focuses on managing and leveraging data and technology resources to support the business and includes IT infrastructure, software development, data analytics, cybersecurity, and digital transformation. Data and technology teams enable efficient operations and data-driven decision-making.

FINANCE AND ACCOUNTING: Manages and reports the company's financial health, directing departments that focus on budgets, financial reports, tax management, payroll, and financial planning and analysis. In regulated industries, it may also include compliance. Finance often manages these functions as well: insurance, real estate and security.

COMMUNICATIONS: Conceives and prepares internal and external communications. Proposes corporate messaging to the public, shareholders, investors, government officials, and employees.

LEGAL: Handles contracts, intellectual property, regulatory compliance, and other legal matters related to the company's interests.

HUMAN RESOURCES (HR): Supports management in acquiring talent, managing talent, onboarding, training and development, performance management, compensation and benefits, and employee relations—all functions intended to foster culture and create a positive work environment.

While you consider job functions and assess postings, you will likely qualify in some respects—for example, good written and verbal communications or adaptability and flexibility (the soft skills). Equally important, if not more important, are the technical skills required—for example, Microsoft Office Suite: Word, Excel, PowerPoint, and Outlook (the hard skills). One way to determine whether you would be interested in a career in any given function would be to focus on the hard skills and ask yourself, "Is this something I would like to learn and develop as an area of expertise?" Look at the mid- and senior-level jobs so you aren't making your judgment based upon the entry-level positions, which by their very nature include a lot of grunt work.

Some career sites list a mix of job functions and industries under the heading "job functions," which is misleading and will confuse your work. So, use the functions I've described as your baseline. The organization chart provided shows how a typical organization is structured.

Think like a scientist—do research, hypothesize, test through further research and follow your own process to choose a job function, and then see what that looks like in your industry of choice. You can research combinations until you find the right one. For example, if the job function of choice is Communications, then look to see how that plays out in a business-to-consumer (B2C) business, such as in the fashion world or a CPG company. Maybe you're interested in product development—look to see how that plays out in a CPG company (B2C) versus a Technology company (B2B or B2C). AI is a good place to start if you want to run through several scenarios. Here's an example of what I got with the following prompt:

"I'm motivated by competence and curiosity. I avoid competition. I need a boss who will provide constructive feedback and give clear direction and guidance. I'm a bit introverted, but I know how to extrovert well. I see the big picture and readily identify themes and patterns. I'm not so good with details. I like variety in my work and jump right in when challenged. I gather information and formulate a logical argument when making recommendations. I did well in school in courses like English, Literature, Art History. I wasn't so good in Math and Science.

I live in New York City and need to launch my career. I'm interested in people, how they behave and what makes them tick. What job functions should I consider?"

Here's the response I received, which is not bad as a starting point:

1. **Human Resources (HR):** Roles like HR coordinator or HR assistant. These positions involve understanding employee needs, managing recruitment processes, and improving workplace culture. Your interest in people and behavior, combined with your ability to see the big picture, would be beneficial here.

2. Market Research Analyst: This role involves studying market conditions, understanding consumer behavior, and identifying trends. Your curiosity and ability to gather information and formulate logical arguments will be valuable in this function.

3. User Experience (UX) Researcher: As a UX researcher, you'll study how users interact with products and services, providing insights to improve user experience. This role combines your interest in behavior with your analytical skills.

4. Communications and Public Relations: Positions like PR assistant or communications coordinator in organizations that focus on understanding and influencing public opinion. These roles involve crafting messages and engaging with the public, aligning with your extroverted abilities and interest in people.

5. Social Work or Counseling: Entry-level roles in social services or counseling centers. These positions allow you to directly work with people, understanding their needs and helping them improve their lives. Your empathy and interest in human behavior are key strengths here.

6. Community Outreach Coordinator: This role involves engaging with community members, organizing events, and understanding community needs. Your ability to see the big picture and connect with people would be beneficial.

7. Training and Development Specialist: As a training specialist, you would design and conduct training programs, helping employees develop skills. This role involves understanding learning behaviors and motivating people, aligning with your interest in human behavior.

The more you can inform AI with data points, the better the results are likely to be, so include information you've learned from taking quizzes, tests, and assessments—and tell it if you prefer a line or staff job. If you can narrow down your choices (e.g., Marketing in B2C in retail), then you can get information about various marketing jobs. Here's the prompt for that: "I'd like to know more about Marketing jobs in a B2C business. What kinds of roles exist?" The response: "In a Business-to-Consumer (B2C) setting, marketing roles are diverse and cater to various aspects of the customer journey. Here are some common marketing roles in B2C businesses:

1. Marketing Coordinator/Assistant: Entry-level role that supports the marketing team with administrative tasks, campaign coordination, and market research.

2. Content Marketing Specialist: Focuses on creating and managing content that engages and attracts customers, such as blog posts, videos, social media updates, and newsletters.

3. Social Media Manager: Manages the company's presence on social media platforms, creating content, engaging with followers, and analyzing performance metrics.

4. Email Marketing Specialist: Develops and executes email marketing campaigns to nurture leads and engage customers, including writing emails, segmenting lists, and analyzing results.

5. SEO/SEM Specialist: Optimizes website content for search engines (Search Engine Optimization/SEO) and manages paid search campaigns (Search Engine Marketing/SEM) to drive traffic and increase visibility.

6. Brand Manager: Oversees the development and maintenance of the brand's image and voice, ensuring consistency across all marketing materials and channels.

7. Digital Marketing Specialist: Focuses on online marketing efforts, including managing digital ad campaigns, analyzing web analytics, and optimizing digital content.

8. Product Marketing Manager: Works closely with product development teams to create marketing strategies for new products, including market research, competitive analysis, and go-to-market plans.

9. Market Research Analyst: Conducts research to understand consumer behavior, market trends, and competitive landscape, providing insights to inform marketing strategies.

10. Customer Relationship Manager (CRM): Manages customer data and interactions to improve customer retention and loyalty through targeted marketing efforts and personalized communication.

11. Influencer Marketing Specialist: Collaborates with influencers and brand ambassadors to promote products and increase brand awareness through authentic and engaging content.

12. Advertising Manager: Plans and executes advertising campaigns across various media channels, including TV, radio, print, and online platforms.

13. Event Marketing Manager: Organizes and promotes events, such as product launches, trade shows, and promotional events, to engage customers and generate leads.

14. Public Relations Specialist: Manages the company's public image and relationships with the media, writing press releases and handling crisis communication.

These roles vary in their focus, but all contribute to creating a comprehensive marketing strategy that attracts, engages, and retains customers in a B2C environment.

If you're not sure about what you want to do, then you may want to test two or three hypotheses and through this research narrow them down to one or two. In this case, rank order the options you're testing and work through all the steps for your first choice. If it works for you, great. If not, go through the steps again with your second choice. My clients often wonder why they shouldn't just work on a couple of ideas at the same time. Think about it this way: if you put 100% of your effort into something, you'll likely get there faster and better. If you only put in 50% effort, then it will take you longer and you might risk losing any momentum you might have had with greater commitment. If you tend to be indecisive, then just choose one and see where it takes you. You'll have the comfort of knowing that if for any reason it doesn't work out, there's always a fallback.

You own the process, so you can do as much or as little research as you want. But in the end you need to choose a job function and industry combination so you can set direction and launch an effective and efficient job search.

You know you're ready to initiate a job search when you have a solid goal statement: "I'm interested in an entry-level position in (function) in the (sector) and specifically in (industry of subsector)."

ORGANIZATION STRUCTURE AND JOB FUNCTIONS

LINE
Revenue generating

General Management

Business Unit Heads

Sales

E-Commerce

Sales Promotion

Marketing

Brand Management

Product Management

Direct Mail

Licensing

Advertising

Affliliate, Partnerships

Sponsorships

Analytics & Data Science

STAFF
Supporting the line positions

Product

Robotics

Plant Management

Manufacturing, Production

Sourcing

Quality Control

Research & Development

Productivity Analysis

Industrial Research

Purchasing

Inventory Management

Distribution

Traffic & Control

Transportation

Packaging / Design

Supply Chain

Information (Data)— Process (Technology)

Systems Analysis & Design

EDP Audit

Project Management

Website Creation

Website Maintenance

Telecommunications

Software Programming

Disaster Recovery

NOTE: Some positions in the product category are more directly related to driving revenue than others. When Designers and Engineers create the product sold, they may be considered line positions.

Cause-Related
Content Management
Influencers
Customer Experience
Digital / Interactive / Social
Events, Experiential
Market Research
Media Buying
Omnichannel

Neuromarketing
Retention & Loyalty Pricing
Telemarketing

Product
Design
Engineering

Information ($)—Profit/ Loss (Financial)
Finance, Accounting, Budgeting
Cash Management, Treasury
Credit & Collection
Tax, Audit, Payroll
Real Estate, Purchasing
Compliance
Insurance
Administration, Facilities, Space Planning
Records
Security

People—External Relationships
Board Support
Communications
   Government relations
   Investor Relations,
   Public Relations
Foundation
Legal, Compliance
Social Responsibility

People—Internal Relationships (Human Resources)
Generalist—Business Partners
Organization Effectiveness
Talent Management
Talent Acquisition (recruitment)
Employee Relations
Compensation & Benefits
Operations, Payroll & HRIS

CHAPTER SIX

Launching:
Initiating Your Job Search with Confidence

Start your job search by targeting prospective organizations and the typical position for which you qualify. With your direction set, the next step is to create a *target list* of prospective organizations within your chosen field. By short-listing organizations, you can directly align your qualifications with what employers seek and prepare to write your résumé and LinkedIn profile.

You might think that researching organizations will delay your getting a job, especially if you feel pressured to get one quickly. Applying to hundreds of jobs online in hopes of getting hired somewhere may be a common approach, but it's not always effective—and creating a target list doesn't have to take too much time (if you have ADHD, trouble with setting or working toward goals, or need to manage learning differences, you can adjust your expectations around how long it will take). In the meantime, consider taking temporary jobs to cover your expenses and student loan. My clients have worked as receptionists, tutors, babysitters, dog walkers, drivers, and retail associates as a way to buy time.

Some clients resist using a list, fearing it will limit their options. But focusing only on current openings means missing out on the hidden job market. By being both strategic and opportunistic, you increase your chances of finding a job. A target list is also a useful tool for networking, transforming your question from "Do you know about any openings?" to "Do you know who knows anything about this company, or do you know someone who would?"

GUIDING PRINCIPLE

To have a sustainable career, be both strategic and opportunistic. When you have a plan, there's a temptation to think you have control of what happens, But if you stick to that plan too rigidly, you might miss out on unexpected opportunities. At the same time, if you only look for career opportunities by pursuing open positions, you may miss out on better jobs because you weren't looking at just the right time. For success, you need to combine both approaches, working toward a goal while seizing opportunities as they present themselves. As with a start–up, it's okay to have a few false starts to explore and get your bearings, but at some point, your business model and path to growth and profitability needs to come together.

In addition, developing your target list educates you about the marketplace and strengthens your candidacy. For example, if you want a job as a software engineer at a tech company, you need to know who the players are, how those companies are structured, their competitive advantage, the basic qualifications needed, and how the recruitment process works. By building up your knowledge and understanding of the sector (industry) and ecosystem in which you want to work, you are better able to align your interests and fortify your candidacy.

TO CREATE YOUR TARGET LIST, FOLLOW THESE STEPS:

STEP 1. Create an industry summary. Highlight on your ecosystem map the place where you want to work. Add a personal statement about why you are interested in working in this specific area. This material will be useful in targeting prospective employers, writing cover letters and preparing for interviews.

STEP 2. Draft a tentative list of fifty to seventy-five target organizations. Choose organizations that interest you. Access lists by revenue and number of employees, best companies to work for, major employers in your area, etc. *Fortune* and *Forbes* have lists by industry. Include large companies even if you prefer smaller ones, as they often have extensive career sections and well-written postings.

STEP 3: Dive deep and assess the tentative targets.
Visit each organization's website to learn about its history, products and/or services, executive team, location, financial results, and career section. Management bios may be found on the website. You can go deeper by reading press releases, white papers and annual reports and listening to podcasts of the leader's or analyst's insights and views. If you read the 10-K report for a publicly held company, you learn about the pay for the most highly compensated executives. (A 10-K report is filed annually with the Securities and Exchange Commission by public companies regarding their financial performance. It includes corporate history and is a tool for investor decision-making.) For nonprofits, find the size of their endowment and assume they earn about 5%, so the annual budget is likely to be about that amount.

LinkedIn is another great resource. View profiles of people who work in your target companies. Compare your list of organizations to where people have worked, particularly where they started. Reading profiles helps you understand the career path that you might be following.

Think about organizational size (larger companies can pay more) and scope of products. What is their history? What do they value—customer service, innovation, diversity? Where is it based? Ideally, you want to work for a company whose HQ is in a location where you are willing to live.

STEP 4: Decide on your target list of thirty to fifty organizations. Targeting thirty to fifty organizations will increase your chances of finding an opening. Too few and your search might be very long; too many and your search will not be focused enough to be productive.

Format your target list so others can review it at a glance, and as with your résumé, put it on one page, with the same font and letterhead so it is a professional presentation. Organize it for easy, user-friendly viewing. For example, you could have categories (buy-side companies, sell-side companies). You could use italics to indicate organizations you've gotten into but where you still need more contacts; you could highlight or boldface those organizations that are priorities for introductions; and so on. Use the list as a communication tool so others can quickly understand the help or connections you're looking for.

Your target list should be updated continually, so track versions by date. Use the list to set weekly goals. Throughout your search, you are educating yourself about these organizations, staying on top of news, and working toward meeting people there who can refer you to current or potential openings.

STEP 5: Target the typical position(s) for which you qualify. Broadly researching the job function is a start, but now you want to narrow your options. You might have an interest in marketing, but that is a large and unwieldy function. You'll need to be more specific and know what kind of work within marketing to target. High-level research looks like this: Use your browser to do an initial search. Type in the job function (e.g., Marketing) and follow the results to get basic information. Wikipedia has good functional descriptions. Some AI programs do a good job, too.

You can search for "job function + company"— for example, "marketing + Johnson & Johnson" and read through current and old postings to get a feel for various marketing positions that exist in a global consumer brand business. Apple, Nike and Amazon write particularly good job descriptions, and they have high qualification standards.

Try to answer questions like these: What do the top (functional) jobs look like? What would be the typical entry-level position that sets you off in this direction? Drill down to the job for which you qualify, what the job title is, and so on, accumulating as much information as you can.

Compensation information is included in postings in many states but not all, so you may need to access sites such as salary.com. Do the organizations on your list tend to pay the same compared to the information you are gathering in networking meetings?

To get the most out of a posting, read it first for an overall understanding and decide if this is a good representation of the job you want. While you're reading through job descriptions, you're learning more and more about what you want to do and how you might be able to create value in that environment. You might read dozens of postings, and when you think you have a good grasp of what most organizations are looking for in candidates, then choose four to six representative examples. If possible, you would ideally have postings from organizations on your target list.

Ask yourself these kinds of questions: Would I enjoy the job? What skills are required? Do I have the potential to be great at that kind of job? How important is that work to the overall objectives of the company? What would I be able to learn in that job? Who would I get to meet? How important is appearance, and would I be comfortable in that role?

Here's an example of a Target List for an individual interested in an entry-level Software Engineer position.

Stephanie Smith

stephanie.smith@gmail.com | 718.456.7890

TARGET LIST *as of (date)*

Technology
Adobe
Apple
Asana
Cisco
Datadog
GitHub
Google
IBM
Lyft
LiveRamp
Microsoft
MongoDB
Notion
NVIDIA
Oracle
Reddit
Rippling
Snap
Twilio

Media / Entertainment / Telecommunications
Comcast (FreeWheel—advertising)
Disney
Netflix

Financial Services
Capital One
ClearStreet
JPM Chase
Plaid
Square
Stripe

Security / Cybersecurity
Clear
Crowdstrike

Defense
Anduril

TARGETED POSITION FOR WHICH I QUALIFY
Software Engineer

STEP 6: Analyze your representative postings for your targeted position (such as Fixed Income Analyst or Human Resources Assistant). Here's a way to analyze these postings:

First, highlight the keywords that may be in the recruiter's formula for identifying qualified candidates. Keywords are the names of relevant people, places or things. For example, "Microsoft Office Suite: Word, Excel, PowerPoint, Outlook." "CRM tools." "Bachelor's degree." You can do this on your computer or print it out and do it with a highlighter.

Next, highlight the action verbs in another color. Focus on the "Responsibilities" section. Notice that most postings use the present tense of verbs (like "manage, provide"), not the past tense or participle (managed, provided or managing, providing, etc.). When you write your accomplishment bullet points in the "Experience" section of your résumé, you want to mimic these verbs but use the past tense because you are citing things you have achieved in the past (even if performed while in your current position).

Finally, review your qualifications. Be honest. Can you check off every requirement? If yes, keep going. If not, what are you missing? Evaluate the importance of what you're missing—is it essential to the position's success? Could you get away with being 80% qualified? Recruiters say that 50% of the people who apply online are not qualified for a given position, so if you're way off the mark, don't bother. But if you're close to being qualified, give it a shot.

If this is a job you really want but don't qualify for, work toward acquiring the missing elements. Get specific about the accomplishment(s) you need to add to your experience. How can you get more value out of your current job so you can qualify in future? For example, if "digital marketing" is a requirement and you are in the process of studying it, then add this to your education section.

STEP 7: Apply your analysis to your résumé and LinkedIn profile. Compare the keywords, action verbs and skills from the postings with your résumé and LinkedIn profile. Will the algorithm and recruiter recognize that you fit their position requirements? With this information in hand, you're now ready to write (or rewrite) your résumé and complete your LinkedIn profile.

Keep in mind that AI is increasingly used to scan résumés, so you may want to test drive your résumé as this technology evolves.

STEP 8: Test your résumé and LinkedIn profile with people in the field you have chosen to validate your success in aligning it with your goal. You've prepared well by reading job postings for the typical position for which you are applying—your best reference, because the job descriptions articulate the qualifications you need to include in your documents. Now it's time to do a reality check to be sure you are market ready. Everyone has an opinion about what makes a good résumé, so you may not want to take all the advice you get. However, it's most important to pay attention to what you hear from recruiters and hiring managers in your chosen field. Tailor and customize your résumé based upon their feedback. For one final pass, ask yourself what you are great at that your résumé doesn't show? Be sure to add it!

Once you have your résumé ready, then you can repurpose your work into your LinkedIn profile. You're now ready to initiate your job search with clarity, confidence and commitment.

Keep in mind that a job search is most effective and has greater long-term value if you are both strategic, which guides your destiny, and opportunistic, which lets you take advantage of what the market is offering at any given time. You control your destiny to the extent that you conduct research and target organizations and typical a position while at the same time spotting online postings that might be open (and appropriate) as you're networking with people you know.

CONCLUSION

This guide was created to help you understand how to set your career direction and launch a search for your first professional job. You now know the questions you must answer to set your career direction. The choices you make will reflect the kind of life and career you want. The goal of this guide is for you to feel clearheaded, confident and committed to moving forward. Please remember that while talent and intellectual capabilities are important, hard work and consistency in the quality of your work are equally, if not more, important. Many people of average capability have achieved unimaginable success through determination, planning and hard work. Whoever you are, whatever you have to offer, an exciting and meaningful future awaits you. Good luck!

Appendix:
Suggested Reading and Key Resources

The following books complement what you have read in *The Work Book*. I hope they might also give you some motivation and inspiration along the way. Most of them have gone through multiple editions, so be sure you're getting the most recent version.

The Artist's Way, **by Julia Cameron** (TarcherPerigee, multiple editions). You might not expect to find a book about creativity in a career guide, but I'm recommending this because it's a timeless and practical approach to overcoming creative blocks, self-doubt, and fear. You need your own voice and creativity to launch your career, and her recommended morning pages for journaling may help you find your confidence and courage.

The Start Up of You, **by Reid Hoffman and Ben Casnocha** (Crown Currency, multiple editions). Reid Hoffman is a cofounder of LinkedIn, so he knows something about networking for jobs. This book explains why you need to manage your career as if you were running a start-up. You'll learn how to be ultracompetitive and face the ever-changing business world.

The Defining Decade: Why Your Twenties Matter—and How to Make the Most of Them Now, **by Meg Jay** (Twelve, multiple editions). Jay is a clinical psychologist and professor who specializes in twentysomethings. She threads neuro research with human development, the value of making intentional, smart decisions in your twenties, and the lifelong impact of those choices.

The Jesuit Guide to (Almost) Everything: A Spirituality for Real Life, **by James Martin, SJ** (HarperOne, 2012). I happen to be a fan of Jim Martin, and while this is not a career or business book, it is a refreshing take on how to manage relationships, money, work, prayer, and decision-making, all while keeping a sense of humor about it. Martin is a Catholic priest, so you have to be willing to read it within the context of applying a spiritual guide to life. Before entering the Jesuits, Jim graduated from the Wharton School of Business.

The Unspoken Rules: Secrets to Starting Your Career Off Right, **by Gorick Ng** (Harvard Business Review Press, 2021). Ng presents a pragmatic, practical guide for first-generation college graduates entering the workforce who do not have family, friends, or sponsors who can give them the necessary, but not explicit, rules of the road.

The 20-Minute Networking Meeting, **by Nathan Perez and Marcia Ballenger, PhD** (Career Innovation Press, 2012, Graduate Edition, 2014). The authors help you learn how to create a networking agenda, lead a networking conversation and be a networker who understands that it is a give-and-take proposition.

To Sell Is Human, **by Daniel Pink** (Riverhead Books, 2013). A great introduction to what sales and selling are about. Pink makes the argument that every job requires the ability to influence and that influence is, in fact, selling.

Learned Optimism, **by Martin E. P. Seligman, PhD** (Vintage, 2006). This is Seligman's initial work, which provides a practical framework for shifting a pessimistic mindset to a more resilient way of thinking. Optimism is not just an innate trait but a learned skill that can help you stay motivated in the face of challenges and enhance your mental health.

The Unspoken Truths for Career Success, **by Tessa White** (HarperCollins Leadership, 2023). White offers an insider's view, having been an HR executive. She decodes management practices for the uninitiated and clearly explains what you need to do to align your interests with those of your

employer.

There are many apps, online programs and tools to help with career development, and new ones are regularly being introduced. But to my knowledge, there is one that has been around for decades, has stood the test of time and remains one of the very best. The Decision Dynamics company, founded by Michael Driver and Kenneth Brousseau, offers help in figuring out the right career path for you. Their instrument, CareerView, is available for a reasonable fee. For a small additional charge, you can engage one of their coaches for personalized guidance. The report shows how your career motives and feelings about work fit with your vision of an ideal career. You can gain insights into how your career should be structured to maximize career satisfaction.

A unique assessment tool is the Kolbe A Index, which measures how people instinctively take action when striving to achieve a goal. It helps you understand how you solve problems, make decisions and get things done when you are free to be yourself. It's not a personality test—use the Myers Briggs for insights about your personality. The Kolbe A Index helps you to identify and articulate your modus operandi around four action modes: Fact Finder (gathering and sharing information), Follow Thru (organizing and designing), Quick Start (dealing with risk and uncertainty) and Implementor (handling space and tangibles). You'll be able to describe your mental energy and how you can best spend it. This tool is available online for a reasonable fee at www.kolbe.com.

LinkedIn is a go-to platform for professionals. Keep in mind that this source provides the most accurate and current information about your school alumni. When you want to find people to network with for career research and job searching, go to your school's Page and click on the Alumni tab. Here you find out where they live, what they do, where they work and what they are skilled at—it's a starting point to initiate contact with people who may be willing to help you learn about your target companies. **85**

To my family and friends, whose support and encouragement have gotten me to the finish line.

To my clients, who have launched their careers, worked hard to develop skills and meaningful work relationships, persisted through growth markets, recessions and pandemics, cared for their families, suffered losses and still come to me for my advice!

To the readers who use this guide to embark on their careers with clarity, confidence and commitment.

And to Cosima, who had absolutely nothing to do with this project but will use this guide when she launches her career in 2042.

ACKNOWLEDGMENTS

I would like to express my heartfelt thanks to the many people who have supported and inspired me. My earliest mentors, Barry Brokaw, who challenged me to start my consulting practice and referred so many amazing people to me; and Sreedhar Menon, who shaped how I approach my work with a respect for the fundamentals. I am indebted to Joan Magretta, who has ingrained competitive advantage into my soul, and Arthur Cinader and Emily Scott, who told me it was my job to put the human into human resources.

This project would not have been completed without the unending support of Jim Larkin, my work colleague, editor, advisor and friend. I am grateful to my first readers, who provided invaluable feedback—Maria Kastanis, Sophia Lewis, Kimberly Farina and Matthew Schnipper. I also thank Ken Brousseau for his help in developing a deeper understanding of how to apply the career path model to today's world.

Clients have asked me to put pen to paper over the years, and many have stayed with me for decades. I greatly appreciate their confidence, trust, and loyalty. Without their generous referrals, my practice wouldn't have been possible. I am especially grateful to Alex Trower and Joan Spero, whose belief in me has been constant and unwavering.

I am deeply grateful to my family—my husband for his courage in supporting my decision to start my consulting practice; my daughter, Allegra, who has taught me about gratitude and resilience; and my son, Nicholas, who has taught me that we can do anything if we believe in ourselves and who frames every obstacle as an opportunity for a work-around.

"Marianne has been essential to my career success in so many ways. From helping me gain a deeper understanding of myself, my skills, values, and goals in my early twenties to navigating the politics of the modern workforce in my thirties, Marianne has been there every step of the way. She has a deep knowledge of various fields, whether it be advancing in your current position or switching careers entirely (both of which I have done!). No matter what you need or where you are in your career path, Marianne is both caring and candid, offering support while being refreshingly honest."
—Alix Eve Schram, Nutritionist

 ISBN: 979-8-9916659-3-3

ABOUT THE AUTHOR

Marianne Ruggiero founded Optima Careers after twenty-five years as a senior human resources executive in New York City and abroad. Her experience covers a range of industries and types of firms, from small entrepreneurial companies to global corporations, from financial services to fashion, including prominent companies such as American Express, Citigroup, and J. Crew. Well versed in nurturing promising talent, Marianne has created staffing, development and coaching programs and accelerated the growth of numerous management teams. She drew on her background to develop the exclusive process she uses with clients today, helping them generate and articulate information about their values, personality, work style and skills to be used in launching and shaping their career and planning life goals. Marianne has contributed to the *Harvard Business Review*, has appeared on CNN Money with Christine Romans and has appeared as a podcast guest with Veronica Dagher of the *Wall Street Journal*.

www.ingramcontent.com/pod-product-compliance
Lightning Source LLC
Chambersburg PA
CBHW040929210326
41597CB00030B/5238